CONTENTS

Mediterranean Grilled Broccoli

Spinach Salad With Tomato Melts

main courses

Curried Chicken Tenders With Honey

Taco Chicken with Creamy Avocado

Chicken with Onion Dates Jam

Citrus Fennel Salad

Cheesy Grilled Tomatoes With Herbs

Juicy Steak with Pineapple Brown Rice

Citrus Beef Ribs With Louisiana Hot Sauce

Sweet Griddle Pork Ribs

Salty Beef Steak

Peppery Strip Steak

Cheesy Griddle Pizza

Chicken With Root Beer

Yellow Chicken Wings Curry

Lobster Tails with Basil & Butter

Dijon Mustard Tender Pork Loin

Hakka Noodles With Smoked Pork Sausage

Cognac Steaks with Shitake Mushrooms

Country-Style Glazed Ribs

Skirt Steak with Coffee Rubbed

Corn Honey-Lime Tilapia

Pineapple Shrimp Skewers

Shrimp Skewers With Pesto Pistachio

Lemon Halibut Fillets with Dill, Spinach & Olives

Spicy Red Snapper Fillets

Rainbow Trout with Cumin and Burnt Citrus Vinaigrette

Chili Crab Legs

Chili Grilled Shrimp

INTRODUCTION

B lackstone Outdoor Gas Griddle is a great and very functional grill that among the search button for years. With this griddle, you can fix the food on it quickly and easily. This is a very useful grill that can make any food you cooked to be delicious. The Blackstone Outdoor Gas Griddle is one of the most fired grills you can find. This grill is easy to clean and this makes it a perfect griddle for your grilling needs. This is also an essential tool for your BBQ cooking because it is very useful when cooking food.

In this cookbook, we have mixed a few of our favorite recipes in the Blackstone Griddle. There are 60 recipes you can have with this griddle. We know that if you are thinking of buying this griddle, you must be questioning yourself, "Is this griddle worth the money?" "Is this griddle worth the trouble?" "How do I use this griddle?"...

So, if you are expecting any kind of answers, the answer would be that the Blackstone Griddle is actually wonderful and that this griddle is a real treat. It offers a wonderful cooking experience that everyone, even a beginner can enjoy cooking their foods. All these questions of yours will be answered here in this cookbook. Today, we're going to share recipes that are from various sources.

The best thing about using griddles is that they are better than your grills in terms of cooking space. Though griddles are smaller when compared to grills, griddles are more useful than many other grills. This is why you should consider using griddles in your cooking if you need to cook related foods. After trying various griddle recipes, we can conclude that there are really great griddle recipes for making delicious foods. These griddle recipes are easy to follow and don't require too many ingredients. The ingredients for these griddle recipes are also more affordable.

BLACKSTONE OUTDOOR GAS GRIDDLE BASICS

The Blackstone griddle is one of the simple and easy to operate outdoor gas griddle manufactured by Blackstone Company. Before we go down to the exciting Blackstone gas griddle recipes, let's get to know first what really a Blackstone Outdoor Gas Griddle, how it works, and everything you need to know to be able to use it.

Blackstone Outdoor Gas Griddle is an item that provides its user with the easiest ways to cook all meals, casseroles, and desserts. There are many kinds of Blackstone Outdoor Gas Griddle in the market and it surely is a challenging job selecting the best type that will deliver you the best cooking experiences. Blackstone Outdoor Gas Griddle is available in different sizes to meet your cooking needs. They have two sizes in total that are the smaller size to cater to 5-1/2 inches diameter cooking area and the bigger size one to cater to 9-1/2 inches diameter cooking area. The Blackstone Outdoor Gas Griddle will fit most of the burners in any size range.

Mainly, the Blackstone griddle is three-sided with two extra sides at the ends. It has a cooking surface of at least 375 square inches and its cooking area can accommodate wide pots, pans, plates, and platters. Its working is all about the gas so it doesn't need any electrical supply, but if you prefer electric burner, there are the electric models as well. It has a cast iron top.

Through the Blackstone Outdoor Gas Griddle, you are able to cook a wide variety of dishes so to make it easier for you to decide what type is best, let us tell you first things first.

The Blackstone Outdoor Gas Griddle is only applicable for non-stick cookware. The cookware also has a slow-heating feature that enables the pans, mugs, and plates to warm up very slowly. Unlike the regular griddle, this allows the heat from the heat source to distribute evenly and this will ensure that all of your cooking items are cooked to the perfect level of temperature.

The Blackstone Outdoor Gas Griddle is made from enamel which is a material that is very durable and heat-leaking. With the enamel material, the griddle naturally protects its surface from scratches, rusts, and chips. In addition, the Blackstone Outdoor Gas Griddle really makes the non-stick coating of the cookware long-lasting and spill-resistant too.

The enamel surface is fully coated with cooking oil and so, nothing can stick to it. Cooking with the Blackstone Outdoor Gas Griddle will make all your cookware non-stick, glazed, and food release from them without having to struggle.

ΔΔΔ

HOW DOES IT WORK?

When you are planning to use the Blackstone Outdoor Gas Griddle, first, you have to get it in conjunction with the cookware that you will be using, then gather all the required materials and foods.

Before you start cooking, of course, you have to check the level of the gas in your grill. First, you need to prepare your cookware to be used. Put the cookware on the right size of the Blackstone. At the back end of the cookware, there is usually a triangle-shaped mark to indicate the gas to be turned on. Turn on the gas by simply twisting the valve and light the burners.

The heat distribution is directly affected by the design of the grill. The Blackstone Outdoor Gas Griddle is just built with the same principle because it has four pothole-shaped patches to make sure that the heat of the burners will be distributed equally to all four sides.

The same principle applies to the classic grills. One of the advantage of the Blackstone Outdoor Gas Griddle is that it is much easier and faster to clean compared to the classic, but it also has a quarter-sized grease-trap inside the work surface.

ΔΔΔ

LET'S TALK ABOUT COOKING

Y ou can cook any kind of foods you want with the Blackstone Outdoor Gas Griddle because it is the perfect casual cookware. It has a cooking surface that is much larger compared to the regular cooking surface so it is best to use all kinds of dishes and accessories.

You can also adjust the temperature and the time of cooking by adjusting the burners. By using the quick release feature, you can let the heat go away without turning the griddle off.

The Blackstone Outdoor Gas Griddle is also applicable for high-heat cooking. You can use it to make rotisserie and low-heat cooking.

ΔΔΔ

HOW TO STORE AND MAINTAIN YOUR

BLACKSTONE OUTDOOR GAS GRIDDLE

L ike the regular grilles, the Blackstone Outdoor Gas Griddle is also very easy to clean. Here we will talk about how to store and maintain your Blackstone Outdoor Gas Griddle properly.

1. Cleaning of the Blackstone Outdoor Gas Griddle

Grilling can be made much easier with the Blackstone Outdoor Gas Griddle. It is just as easy to clean as the regular grilles. Just wipe the griddle clean and keep it away from the rain and stay away from the heat source in any weather. If you need to thoroughly clean the griddle, you can use a stiff-bristled brush to do it. You also need not use too much soap to clean your outdoor gas griddle. To preserve the Blackstone Outdoor Gas Griddle for a longer time, you can wipe it with a soft cloth to remove the dust and grime on it. After that, you can also give it a little bit of water and let it dry thoroughly outside. It has a waterproof coat, but by using a little bit of water, you can wash off the excess oil. Make sure it is kept away from hitting the floor and the cupboards. The enamel surface of the griddle will be scratched easily.

2. Storage of the Blackstone Outdoor Gas Griddle

To make it best for storing, first, make sure that the burners are off and the heat source is down. Store in an area that is not reachable to children and pets to avoid severe accidents. This will help your Blackstone Outdoor Gas Griddle last longer without getting scratches or any physical damage.

ΔΔΔ

BENEFITS OF USING THIS KIND OF GRIDDLE

The Blackstone gas griddle is one of the best choices for your outdoor weekend parties. Here are the major benefits of using this kind of griddle. 1. Most of the food your family eats is prepared in this kind of griddle. So, you have to make sure that you have the best griddle on your list. Cooking with a gas griddle is considered best.

2. You as a cook in your family can use it to prepare different dishes with various flavors.

The griddle can be your source to get an occasion better.

3. Blackstone grills have storage tables that can be spread in a convenient manner.

You can easily organize the ingredients and you do not have to be with no proper food for a long time.

4. There is a good airflow circulation in the Blackstone griddle.

This will ensure that all the food emits the freshest flavor.

5. There is a very convenient material, enamel in this kind of griddle.

You will not have to be concerned about the longevity of the griddle because its surface is scratch-resistant and heat-resistant. This can help in preserving its youth.

6. The heavy-duty cast-iron surface of this type of griddle is very sturdy and it does not have to be fixed on the table as it is removable.

7. There is a versatile grill that can be used for a variety of cooking purposes.

It is also easy to clean and maintain.

8. Blackstone griddle can help you save money if you are not willing to buy all gaiters and griddles that are available in the market.

The Blackstone griddle will make your life and love cooking much more enjoyable. You will not be able to find another griddle that will be as impressive or appealing as this. It has the finest features to enable you to cook your favorite dish perfectly. You can easily experiment with a lot of dishes for your family.

ΔΔΔ

BEST GRIDDLE TOOLS TO USE

When cooking with the Blackstone griddle there are some tools that can help you do it faster and easier. You can try any of the following tools:

1. Spatula:

It is a kind of a spoon and it is used to stir the foods and scrape the food from the griddle. It is made from a plastic material that is heat-resistant chip-resistant and break-resistant.

2. Tongs:

It is a tool that will help you protect your hands from the heat of the gas griddle. It is made from metal that is long and is one of the best tools to use on the Blackstone griddle.

3. Chafing Dish:

It is a tool that cannot be missed on this type of griddle. You can use it to prepare any kind of dishes. You have to make sure that your dishes are hot enough so that they can be used. You have to have an ample amount of hot water for chafing.

4. Rotisserie:

It is an accessory that is used to hold the food item and turn it easily. It is commonly made from metal and very much effective in cooking.

5. Stirring Tools:

You can use it for any kind of food that has to be prepared slowly and effectively on your griddle. It will be easier to use this over the tong.

6. Scrapper Tool:

It is a device that is used for scraping the food from the Blackstone griddle. It is also made out of metal and very effective in preparing all types of food. The main use of the scraper tool is for digging and scrapping purposes. It is used to clean the top cooking surface for derbies and also use to lift cake, pie, pizza, and tarts.

7. Squeeze Bottles:

It is commonly known as condiment bottles. It is used for the condiments used for eating all types of food. It is made from a squeezable and leak-proof material.

8. Tea Kettle:

It is made for making hot water for tea. When it is hot it is very convenient to use it for tea. You can also use it for hot water when you are preparing your food on the grill. It has a safety lock to prevent any accidents.

With all the tools that you can use, you can cook any food with more effectiveness and efficiency. If you are a beginner in using this kind of griddle, it is highly advised that you use the above tools in order to make it easier for you to get used to it.

TIPS AND TRICKS TO USE IT IN THE BEST WAY

H ere are some important tips and tricks for you to use properly the Blackstone Griddle.

1. Season Grill Cooking Surface Regularly

It is best to season your Blackstone griddle before using it for the first time. Seasoning the grill will help the seasoning to stick around and will stick to your foods that are being prepared. The season can prevent the foods from adhering to the griddle. You can prepare your Blackstone griddle by preheating it over the direct heat to approximately 450 degrees Fahrenheit.

2. Use A Proper Oil While Cooking

The key to cooking the food with a griddle, even in a Blackstone griddle, is to make sure that it is with an oil. The oil will make sure that the food will not stick while it is being cooked.

3. Use Liners

When you are using a gas griddle, it will help you to cook by making the food that you want to prepare stick less to the surface.

4. Take Good Care Of Them

The griddles may get damaged in some way. It is best to check for signs of wear and tear. If you find any damage on the griddle, there are some ways you can take care of it. You can polish the griddle with a stainless steel polish. It is important to polish them regularly to keep the grill shiny. The more your griddle is polished, the more the quality of cooking will be.

5. Use Long-Handled Tongs

You can use the long-handled tongs when you are cooking with the Blackstone griddle. It is very useful in protecting your hands from getting the heat from the griddle.

6. Be Sure To Have Enough Water Ready

It is best for you to have enough water to be ready and prepared. You should not cook without having water or cooking oil. The hot water is the best way to make the food that you will be cooking have the freshest flavor.

7. Do Not Disturb The Browning

If you are putting the food on a griddle in order to make browning, do not disturb it. Disturbing your food will make it so it will not brown as it should. You should leave it to be on its own for browning.

8. Let The Food Sit for Longer

If you are cooking on a Blackstone grill, you should let the food sit on the grill for a little bit longer to enjoy the taste of the food.

As you can see, Blackstone Outdoor Gas Griddles are very useful and helpful and, if you decide to have one, surely it will prepare you all kinds of cooking, breakfast, lunch, dinner, and snacks that can all be cooked just through fire. There's no need for electricity as well. So, be spontaneous and have fun with the griddle.

ΔΔΔ

HOW TO SEASON YOUR GRIDDLE BEFORE USE

You can easily season your griddle with some preparation. In order to season your griddle, you can use some oil and some kind of fat. We will look at some major types of oil you can use, and you can also have more preparation, and your griddle will be ready to use.

1. Apply an oil-based seasoning on a gas grill cooking surface using a microfiber cloth.

You can use any type of oil to season your griddle. Some of the best oils that can be used are the ones from coconut oil, canola oil, grapeseed oil, corn oil, and vegetable oil. Make sure that the oil you are using is unrefined and unfiltered.

2. Apply a layer of oil to the grill griddle using a clean cloth.

You can have a layer of oil on your griddle by using this. You can easily make a layer of oil using the oil-based seasoning that you spread on your griddle. Make sure that you are using more layers of oil so that it will be easier for the food to get a better flavor.

3. Let the oil-based seasoning dry. You should not use too much of what you have on it.

When you are using the oil-based seasoning on the gas griddle, you should not use more than what you have used. You should let it dry properly to avoid the food from getting wet from it.

4. Remove the layer of oil to avoid the food from getting wet and having an oily texture.

You can remove the layer of oil on the griddle to avoid it from getting wet. You can easily remove it by using a scraper or a spatula. Once you remove it, you should use a clean cloth to wipe it.

5. Prepare a very it layers on the gas grill cooking surface using a microfiber cloth.

You can prepare a very little layer on your griddle for you to be able to avoid the food that you want to cook from sticking.

When you are taking care of your griddle, you should already know how to take care of it. You should know how to take care of the food that you cook on it. If you are able to prepare some good foods on it, the griddle will be happy for you. It will last longer and you will not have to change it.

You can make the griddle last up to several years if you are taking good care of it. By regularly cleaning it and keeping it polished and oiled regularly, it will last longer.

BREAKFAST RECIPES

PEANUT BUTTER GRAPE JELLY PANCAKE

Preparation time: 5 minutes | Cooking time: 5 minutes | Griddle Temperature: medium heat | Servings: 4

Ingredients:

Pancakes:

- 2 eggs
- 1 ½ cups whole milk ½ cup smooth peanut butter
- 1 ¼ cups pancake mix

Peanut Butter Cream:

- ½ cup smooth peanut butter
- 1 (8-oz.) container whipped topping

Grape Syrup:

- ¼ cup grape jelly
- ½ cup maple syrup

Directions:

1. Preheat the griddle pan over medium heat. Make pancake batter: Beat together the egg and milk. Add the peanut butter and beat until smooth. Mix in the pancake mix.
2. For your peanut buttercream, mix the peanut butter plus whipped topping. For the grape syrup, combine the jelly and syrup. Microwave until melted, about 20 seconds. Mix to combine.
3. Ladle a half cup of the pancake batter onto the pan. Cook until golden brown, about 2 minutes per side. Continue until all batter is used up.
4. Stack the pancakes, spreading a smear of the peanut buttercream between each pancake. Spry with the grape syrup before serving.

Nutrition:

- Calories: 320
- Carbs: 36g
- Fat: 17g
- Protein: 10g

FRENCH TOAST WITH MELTED VANILLA ICE CREAM

Preparation time: 5 minutes | Cooking time: 8 minutes | Griddle Temperature: medium-high heat | Servings: 4

Ingredients:

- 1 cup vanilla ice cream, melted
- 3 eggs
- 1 tsp vanilla extract
- the ground cinnamon, as needed
- 8 slices Texas toast/other thick-cut bread
- Cooking oil, as needed

Directions:

1. Mix the melted ice cream, eggs, vanilla extract, plus cinnamon in a bowl wide until frothy.

2. Set the griddle grill to medium-high heat, then coat the surface using oil. Dip each side of the bread into your prepared batter.
3. Put the bread on your griddle, then grill within 3 to 4 minutes on each side. Repeat with the remaining fixings, and serve.

Nutrition:

- Calories: 487
- Carbs: 43g
- Fat: 15g
- Protein: 45g

BRIOCHE WITH CINNAMON FRENCH TOAST

Preparation time: 10 minutes | Cooking time: 3-4 minutes | Griddle
Temperature: medium heat | Servings: 6

Ingredients:

- 10 eggs
- ¾ cup half and half
- 2 tsp. cinnamon
- 1 tsp. almond extract
- ¼ cup maple syrup, to serve
- 1 loaf brioche bread, sliced

Directions:

1. In a bowl, whisk the eggs well. Mix in half and half, cinnamon, and almond extract. Soak bread in the egg batter for 5 minutes.
2. Preheat the griddle pan on medium heat, 3-4 minutes. Melt 2 tbsp butter onto the pan. Cook the French toast to the desired doneness. Repeat

until all are cooked. Serve with maple syrup.

Nutrition:

- Calories: 200
- Carbs: 8g
- Fat: 5g
- Protein: 2

SPICY BACON BURRITO WITH POTATO & AVOCADO

Preparation time: 10 minutes | Cooking time: 20 minutes | Griddle
Temperature: medium-high heat | Servings: 2

Ingredients:

- 4 eggs
- 4 strips bacon
- 1 russet potato, large, peeled & cut into small cubes
- 1 red bell pepper
- ½ yellow onion
- 1 ripe avocado, sliced
- 2 tablespoon hot sauce
- 2 large flour tortillas
- Vegetable oil

Directions:

1. Preheat the griddle to medium-high heat on one side and medium heat on the other side. Brush with vegetable oil and add the bacon to the

medium heat side and peppers and onions to the medium-high side.

2. When the bacon finishes cooking, place on paper towels and chop into small pieces. Add the potatoes to the bacon fat on the griddle. Cook the potatoes until softened.

3. Add the eggs to the vegetable side and cook until firm. Place the ingredients onto the tortillas and top with slices of avocado and a tablespoon of hot sauce. Fold the tortillas and enjoy.

Nutrition:

- Calories: 541
- Carbs: 33g
- Fat: 20g
- Protein: 25g

GRUYERE OMELET WITH BACON

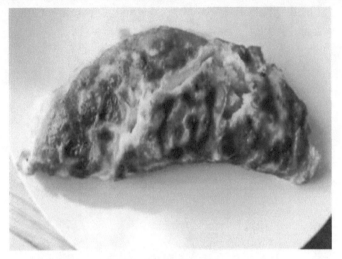

Preparation time: 5 minutes | Cooking time: 15 minutes | Griddle
Temperature: medium heat | Servings: 2

Ingredients:

- 6 eggs, beaten
- 6 strips bacon
- ¼ pound Gruyere, shredded
- 1 teaspoon black pepper
- 1 teaspoon salt
- 1 tablespoon chives, finely chopped
- Vegetable oil

Directions:

1. Add salt to the beaten eggs and set aside for 10 minutes. Heat your griddle to medium heat and add the bacon strips.
2. Cook until most of the fat has rendered, but bacon is still flexible. Remove the bacon from the griddle and place it on paper towels. Once

the bacon has drained, chop it into small pieces.

3. Add the eggs to the griddle in two even pools. Cook until the bottom of the eggs starts to firm up.
4. Add the gruyere to the eggs and cook until the cheese has started to melt and the eggs are just starting to brown.
5. Add the bacon pieces and use a spatula to turn one half of the omelet onto the other half. Remove from the griddle, season with pepper and chives, and serve.

Nutrition:

- Calories: 249
- Carbs: 2g
- Fat: 19g
- Protein: 24g

SCRAMBLED EGG WITH TOMATO & BASIL

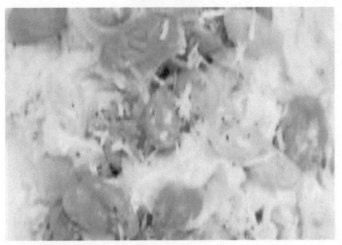

Preparation time: 10 minutes | Cooking time: 5 minutes | Griddle
Temperature: medium heat | Servings: 2

Ingredients:

- 2 eggs, lightly beaten
- 2 tbsp fresh basil, chopped
- 1 tbsp olive oil
- 1/2 tomato, chopped
- Pepper, to taste
- Salt, to taste

Directions:

1. Preheat the griddle to medium heat. Add oil on top of the griddle. Add tomatoes and cook until softened.
2. Whisk eggs with basil, pepper, and salt. Pour egg mixture on top of

tomatoes and cook until eggs are set. Serve and enjoy.

Nutrition:

- Calories 125
- Fat 12 g
- Carbohydrates 1 g
- Protein 5.8 g

BANANA PEANUT BUTTER SUNDAE

Preparation time: 5 minutes | Cooking time: 5 minutes | Griddle Temperature: high heat | Servings: 4

Ingredients:

- 4 bananas, peeled & sliced into medallions
- Cinnamon powder, as needed
- Cayenne pepper, as needed
- 4 large scoops of vanilla ice cream
- ½ cup creamy peanut butter
- Caramel sauce, as needed
- Peanuts, chopped, as needed
- Salted Caramel Peanut Butter Sundae
- Pink sea salt, as needed

Directions:

1. Sprinkle the bananas with cinnamon and cayenne pepper before grilling

for a little kick!

2. Grill bananas on high heat. Scoop ice cream into a serving bowl. Top with bananas, then peanut butter, caramel sauce, and chopped peanuts.

3. Sprinkle lightly with pink sea salt before serving—½ cup caramel sauce ¼ cup peanuts, chopped pink sea salt, to sprinkle.

Nutrition:

- Calories: 170
- Carbs: 28g
- Fat: 5g
- Protein: 4g

SCRAMBLED EGG WITH BLACK BEANS & CHORIZO

Preparation time: 5 minutes | Cooking time: 10 minutes | Griddle
Temperature: medium heat| Servings: 4

Ingredients:

- 8 eggs, beaten
- 1 pound Chorizo
- ½ yellow onion
- 1 cup cooked black beans
- ½ cup green chilies
- ½ cup jack cheese
- ¼ cup green onion, chopped
- ½ teaspoon black pepper
- Vegetable oil

Directions:

1. Preheat a griddle to medium heat. Brush your griddle using vegetable oil and add the chorizo to one side and the onions to the other side.
2. When the onion has softened, combine it with the chorizo and add the beans and chilies. Add the eggs, cheese, and green onion and cook until eggs have reached desired firmness.
3. Remove the scramble from the griddle and season with black pepper before serving.

Nutrition:

- Calories: 129
- Carbs: 2g
- Fat: 7g
- Protein: 10g

CHEESY BACON & EGG SANDWICH

Preparation time: 5 minutes | Cooking time: 10 minutes | Griddle
Temperature: medium heat | Servings: 4

Ingredients:

- 4 large eggs
- 8 strips of bacon
- 4 slices cheddar or American cheese
- 8 slices sourdough bread
- 2 tablespoons butter
- 2 tablespoons vegetable oil

Directions:

1. Heat your griddle to medium heat and place the strips of bacon on one side. Cook until just slightly crispy.

2. When the bacon is nearly finished, place the oil on the other side of the griddle and crack with eggs onto the griddle. Cook them either sunny side up or over medium.
3. Butter one side of each slices of your bread and place them butter side down on the griddle.
4. Place a slice of cheese on 4 of the slices of bread and when the cheese has just started to melt, and the eggs are finished, stack the eggs on the bread.
5. Add the bacon to the sandwiches and place the other slice of bread on top. Serve immediately.

Nutrition:

- Calories: 310
- Carbs: 7g
- Fat: 22g
- Protein: 19g

VEGETABLES RECIPES

POLENTA WITH ROSEMARY

Preparation time: 5 minutes | Cooking time: 10 minutes | Griddle
Temperature: high heat | Servings: 4-6

Ingredients:

- 24-oz. log prepared polenta
- 2 teaspoon extra-virgin olive oil
- garlic salt to taste
- lemon pepper to taste
- 2 tablespoons chopped rosemary

Directions:

1. Preheat Griddle on high. Cut the polenta into 12½-inch thick slices. Place the slices on a baking sheet.
2. Brush both sides of the polenta rounds with oil and season lightly with garlic salt, lemon pepper, and sprinkle with chopped rosemary leaves. Lightly oil the grill rack and.
3. Grill your polenta slices over high heat until nicely browned, within 3 to 5 minutes per side. Remove from heat and serve on a heated platter.

Nutrition:

- Calories: 71
- Carbs: 16g
- Fat: 1g
- Protein: 2g

GRIDDLE LEEKS

Preparation time: 6 minutes | Cooking time: 14 minutes | Griddle
Temperature: medium-low heat | Servings: 4

Ingredients:

- 4 leeks (1–1½ pounds)
- Salt and pepper, as needed
- olive oil, as needed

Directions:

1. Heat a Griddle for medium to medium-low heat. Trim the root ends of your leeks and cut away the tough green tops.
2. Make a long vertical slit through the center of the leek from the root end through the remaining green part, but not cutting through to the other side. Rinse well to get the sand out from between the layers. Sprinkle both sides with salt.
3. Open up the leeks and Place them on the grill directly, cut side down,

pressing down gently with a spatula to make sure the layers fan out
over the heat.
4.   Cook until they have fully softened, 6 to 8 minutes, depending on their
     thickness. Brush with some oil, turn and cook until the bottom browns,
     1 to 3 minutes.
5.   Brush the top using oil, turn, then cook for another 1 to 3 minutes.
     Transfer the leeks to a plate, sprinkle with pepper, and serve hot, warm,
     or room temperature.

Nutrition:

- Calories: 63
- Carbs: 9g
- Fat: 3g
- Protein: 1g

GRILLED OKRA

Preparation time: 5 minutes | Cooking time: 5-10 minutes | Griddle
Temperature: medium heat | Servings: 4

Ingredients:

- 1½ pounds okra pods, stem ends trimmed
- 2 tablespoons good-quality olive oil
- 2 teaspoons coarse sea salt

Directions:

1. Heat a Griddle for medium heat. Place the okra in a bowl. Spry with the oil and toss to coat completely. Sprinkle with the salt and toss again.
2. Place the okra on the grill directly. Cook it while turning them once or twice, until the pods turn bright green within 5 to 10 minutes. Transfer to your platter and serve hot or at room temperature.

Nutrition:

- Calories: 27
- Carbs: 6g
- Fat: 0g
- Protein: 2g

GRIDDLE PLUM-TOMATOES

Preparation time: 5 minutes | Cooking time: 1-3 hours | Griddle Temperature: medium-low heat | Servings: 4

Ingredients:

- 4 plum tomatoes
- olive oil for brushing
- Salt and pepper, as needed

Directions:

1. Heat a Griddle for medium to low indirect. Cut the tomatoes in half lengthwise. Brush them with oil and sprinkle the cut sides with salt and pepper.
2. Place the tomatoes on the indirect side of the grill, cut side up. If the temperature is closer to medium, keep the tomatoes some distance from the heat to avoid charring.

3. Close the grill and cook until shriveled, but you can still see signs of moisture, at least 1 hour and up to 3 hours.
4. About halfway through, move and rotate the tomatoes, so they cook evenly. Transfer to your platter and serve hot.

Nutrition:

- Calories: 100
- Carbs: 16g
- Fat: 1g
- Protein: 5g

GLAZED TOFU STEAKS WITH MANGO SALSA

Preparation time: 10 minutes + marinating time | Cooking time: 4-5 minutes | Griddle Temperature: medium heat | Servings: 4-6

Ingredients:

- 1 bunch fresh cilantro
- 2/3 cup white vegetable stock (below)
- ¼ cup lemon juice
- 1 tablespoon crushed red pepper
- ¼ cup minced fresh ginger
- 1 tablespoon brown sugar
- 1 teaspoon blackstrap molasses
- 5 garlic cloves

- black pepper, to taste
- 1 small fresh pineapple
- 2 mangos
- 1 ¼ pound firm tofu, drained, cut lengthwise into four 1-inch thick "steaks."

Directions:

1. Chop the cilantro to make ½ cup and set aside 1 tablespoon of it for salsa.
2. In a medium-sized baking dish, combine the chopped cilantro and the stock, lemon juice, red pepper, ginger, sugar, molasses, garlic, and black pepper. Mix and add the tofu.
3. Marinate it for 2 hours at room temperature. Peel the pineapple and mangos, then finely chop, discard pineapple skin and core, and mango skin and pit.
4. Combine the fruit and 1 tablespoon of the reserved chopped cilantro in a medium serving bowl. Set it aside at room temperature to let the flavors combine.
5. Prepare the outdoor griddle for medium heat Drain tofu, reserving marinade.
6. Lightly oil grill and place tofu on grill over griddle the tofu until lightly browned, 4-5 minutes, frequently brushing with the marinade and turning once. Serve the tofu steaks with the pineapple and mango mixture.

Nutrition:

- Calories: 138
- Carbs: 7g
- Fat: 9g
- Protein: 8g

RATATOUILLE

Preparation time: 15 minutes | Cooking time: 26 minutes | Griddle
Temperature: medium-high heat | Servings: 6-8

Ingredients:

- 1 red onion, cut into ½-inch-thick slices, and skewered
- 2 pounds eggplant, sliced into ¾-inch-thick rounds
- 1½ pounds zucchini or summer squash, sliced lengthwise into ½-inch-thick planks
- 2 bell peppers, stemmed, seeded, and halved, each half cut into thirds
- 1 pound tomatoes, cored and halved
- ¼ cup extra-virgin olive oil, plus extra for brushing
- Salt and pepper, to taste
- 3 tablespoons sherry vinegar
- ¼ cup chopped fresh basil
- 1 tablespoon minced fresh thyme

- 1 garlic clove, minced to paste

Directions:

1. Place onion, eggplant, zucchini, bell peppers, and tomatoes on a baking sheet, brush with oil, and season with salt and pepper. Whisk ¼ cup oil, vinegar, basil, thyme, and garlic in a large bowl.
2. Turn all your burners to high, cover, then heat the grill until hot, within 15 minutes. Turn all burners to medium-high.
3. Place vegetables on grill and cook, turning once, until tender and streaked with grill marks, 10 to 12 minutes for onion, 8 to 10 minutes for eggplant and squash, 7 to 9 minutes for peppers, and 4 to 5 minutes for tomatoes. Remove vegetables and let cool slightly.
4. Chop the vegetables into ½-inch pieces and add to oil mixture; toss to coat. Season with salt plus pepper to taste, and serve warm or at room temperature.

Nutrition:

- Calories: 189
- Carbs: 15g
- Fat: 12g
- Protein: 3g

MEDITERRANEAN GRILLED BROCCOLI

Preparation time: 10 minutes | Cooking time: 6 minutes | Griddle
Temperature: high heat| Servings: 6

Ingredients:

- 4 cups broccoli florets
- 1 1/2 tsp garlic, minced
- 1 1/2 tsp Italian seasoning
- 1 tbsp lemon juice
- 4 tbsp olive oil
- 1/4 tsp pepper
- 1 1/4 tsp kosher salt

Directions:

1. Add broccoli and remaining ingredients into the bowl and mix well.

Cover and place in the refrigerator for 1 hour—Preheat the griddle to high heat.

2. Spray griddle top with cooking spray. Place broccoli florets on a hot griddle top and cook for 3 minutes on each side. Serve and enjoy.

Nutrition:

- Calories 106
- Fat 9.9 g
- Carbohydrates 4.5 g
- Protein 1.8 g

SPINACH SALAD WITH TOMATO MELTS

Preparation time: 5 minutes | Cooking time: 6 minutes | Griddle Temperature: medium-high heat | Servings: 4

Ingredients:

- 1 or 2 large fresh tomatoes (enough for 4 thick slices across)
- 2 tablespoons good-quality olive oil, plus more for brushing
- Salt and pepper
- 2 teaspoons white wine vinegar
- 1 teaspoon Dijon mustard
- 3 cups baby spinach
- 6 slices cheddar cheese (about 4 ounces)

Directions:

1. Core the tomatoes and cut 4 thick slices (about 1 inch); save the

trimmings. Brush them using oil and sprinkle with salt and pepper on both sides.
2. Whisk the 2 tablespoons of oil, vinegar, and mustard together in a bowl. Chop the trimmings from the tomatoes; add them to the dressing along with the spinach, and toss until evenly coated.
3. Set the griddle grill to medium-high heat. Oil your griddle and allow it to heat until the oil is shimmering but not smoking. Put the tomato slices and cook for 3 minutes.
4. Turn the tomatoes, top each slice with a slice of cheddar, and cook until the cheese is melted 2 to 3 minutes. Transfer to plates and serve with the salad on top.

Nutrition:

- Calories: 121
- Carbs: 17g
- Fat: 15g
- Protein: 8g

MAIN COURSES

CURRIED CHICKEN TENDERS WITH HONEY

Preparation time: 15 minutes | Cooking time: 10-12 minutes | Griddle
Temperature: medium-high heat | Servings: 4

Ingredients:

- 1 lb. chicken tenders, cut into finger-thick slices
- 1/2 cup honey
- 1/3 cup dark soy sauce
- 3 tbsps. olive oil
- 1 tbsp. paprika
- 2 tbsps. curry powder
- Salt and pepper to taste

Directions:

1. Preheat your griddle to medium-high. Mix the soy sauce, paprika, curry powder, honey, plus olive oil in a bowl. Dump in the chicken and mix. Season with salt plus pepper to taste.
2. Let the mixture stand within 10-15 minutes. Place on the griddle to cook halfway through. Remove from flat top and transfer to a roasting pan and spread evenly so that the chicken pieces are just 1 layer.
3. Cover with aluminum foil and place roasting pan back on a flat top until fully cooked through. Approximately 10 – 12 minutes. Garnish with spring onion, and enjoy!

Nutrition:

- Calories: 619
- Fat: 13g
- Carbs: 39g
- Protein: 4g

TACO CHICKEN WITH CREAMY AVOCADO

Preparation time: 20 minutes | Cooking time: 10 minutes | Griddle
Temperature: medium heat | Servings: 4-5

Ingredients:

- 1 (½ pound) Boneless, skinless chicken breasts, sliced thin

The Chicken Marinade:

- 1 serrano pepper, minced
- 2 teaspoons garlic, minced
- 1 lime, juiced
- 1 teaspoon ground cumin
- ⅓ cup olive oil

- Sea salt, to taste
- Black pepper, to taste

Creamy Avocado:

- 1 cup sour cream
- 2 teaspoons lime juice
- 1 teaspoon lime zest
- 1 serrano pepper, diced and seeded
- 1 clove garlic, minced
- 1 large hass avocado

The Garnish:

- ½ cup queso fresco, crumbled
- 2 teaspoons cilantro, chopped
- 1 lime sliced into wedges
- 10 corn tortillas

Directions:

1. Mix chicken marinade in a sealable plastic bag. Add chicken and toss to coat well. Marinate for 1 hour in the refrigerator.
2. Combine the creamy avocado fixings in a food processor or blender and pulse until smooth. Cover then refrigerate until you are ready to assemble tacos.
3. Preheat griddle to medium heat and grill chicken for 5 minutes per side; rotating and turning as needed.
4. Remove from griddle and tent loosely with aluminum foil. Allow chicken to rest for 5 minutes. Serve with warm tortillas, a dollop of avocado crema, queso fresco, cilantro, and lime wedges.

Nutrition:

- Calories: 213
- Carbs: 26g
- Fat: 6g
- Protein: 17g

CHICKEN WITH ONION DATES JAM

Preparation time: 15 minutes | Cooking time: 40-45 minutes | Griddle
Temperature: medium heat| Servings: 4

Ingredients:

- 4 skin-on chicken legs, including thighs
- Salt, for coating

Onion and Smoked Date Jam:

- 2 unpeeled red onions, halved
- Oil, honey, and salt, for coating
- 6 pitted dates, smoked
- ½ cup sugar
- 1 cup vinegar
- 1 cup water

Directions:

1. Wipe your griddle surface using oil to prevent sticking. Set a medium-heat. Rub your chicken legs using a light coating of salt and let them sit at room temperature for 30 minutes.
2. For the jam, toss the onions in oil, honey, and salt to coat. Grill, slice side down on medium heat until well charred, about 5 minutes.
3. Transfer to a plate, set aside until cool enough to handle, then peel and thinly slice and add to a saucepan.
4. Coarsely chop the dates and add to the saucepan along with the sugar, vinegar, and water. Put on medium heat and simmer until reduced and deeply caramelized for about 45 minutes.
5. While the jam reduces, grill the chicken legs over medium heat, turning every 5 minutes.
6. Transfer it to your cutting board and let rest for 10 minutes before cutting the thighs from the drumsticks. Serve immediately with the jam.

Nutrition:

- Calories: 290
- Carbs: 72g
- Fat: 0g
- Protein: 1g

CITRUS FENNEL SALAD

Preparation time: 10 minutes | Cooking time: 10 minutes | Griddle
Temperature: medium heat | Servings: 4-6

Ingredients:

- ½ cup rice vinegar
- ¼ cup sugar
- 1 small red onion, halved, thinly sliced, and pulled apart
- 2 pounds fennel
- 2 tablespoons olive oil, + more for brushing
- 3 navel oranges
- 1 teaspoon minced fresh rosemary
- Salt and pepper

Directions:

1. Put the vinegar plus sugar in a small nonreactive saucepan and bring to a boil. Remove, then put the onion, and mix to combine.
2. Or you can do this earlier in the day, cover, and let sit at room temperature. Heat a Griddle for medium heat.

3. Trim the fennel bulbs, reserving the feathery fronds. Cut the fennel in half from stalk end to base; brush with some oil.
4. Cut the peel from your oranges with a small knife, deep enough to remove the white pith. Slice the oranges across into ¼-inch rounds, then cut the rounds into wedges. Place in a large bowl. Place the fennel on the grill directly.
5. Turning once, until the fennel is crisp-tender and browned or charred in spots, 3 to 5 minutes per side. Transfer it to a cutting board and thinly slice it across into crescents. Add to the oranges.
6. Use a slotted spoon to transfer the onion to the bowl; reserve the brine. Mince enough fennel fronds to make 2 tablespoons.
7. Add the oil, 1 tablespoon of the brine, the rosemary, the minced fronds, and some salt and pepper. Toss to coat, taste and adjust the seasoning, and serve.

Nutrition:

- Calories: 113
- Carbs: 23g
- Fat: 0g
- Protein: 2g

CHEESY GRILLED TOMATOES WITH HERBS

Preparation time: 5 minutes | Cooking time: 10 minutes | Griddle
Temperature: medium heat | Servings: 4

Ingredients:

- 3 or 4 fresh tomatoes (1½ pounds)
- olive oil for brushing
- Salt and pepper
- 1/3 cup or more torn or chopped fresh basil leaves
- Freshly grated Parmesan cheese (optional)

Directions:

1. Heat a griddle for medium heat. Core the tomatoes and cut each across into 3 or 4 thick slices. Brush them with oil and sprinkle with salt and pepper on both sides.
2. Place the tomato slices on the grill directly. Cook it while turning once,

until they are soft but not mushy, 3 to 5 minutes per side.

3.   Transfer the slices to a platter, sprinkle with basil and some cheese if you like, and serve hot, warm, or at room temperature.

Nutrition:

- Calories: 110
- Carbs: 5g
- Fat: 8g
- Protein: 4g

JUICY STEAK WITH PINEAPPLE BROWN RICE

Preparation time: 10 minutes | Cooking time: 10 minutes | Griddle
Temperature: medium-high heat | Servings: 4

Ingredients:

- 4 (4-ounce) beef fillets
- ¼ cup soy sauce
- ½ teaspoon black pepper
- ½ teaspoon garlic powder
- 1 (8 oz) can of pineapple chunks, in juice, drained
- 2 scallions, thin sliced
- 2 (8.8-ounce) packages of pre-cooked brown rice, like Uncle Ben's
- 7/8 teaspoon kosher salt

- Olive oil, for brushing

Directions:

1. Combine soy sauce, pepper, garlic powder, and beef in a large sealable plastic bag. Seal and massage sauce into beef; let stand at room temperature for 7 minutes, turning bag occasionally.
2. Preheat griddle to medium-high heat and brush with olive oil. Add pineapple and green onions to grill and cook 5 minutes or well charred, turning to char evenly.
3. Remove pineapple mix and brush with additional olive oil. Add steaks and cook 3 minutes on each side, for rare, or until the desired temperature is reached.
4. Cook rice according to package instructions. Add rice, pineapple, onions, and salt to a bowl and stir gently to combine. Plate steaks with pineapple rice and serve!

Nutrition:

- Calories: 369
- Fat: 12.4g
- Carbs: 37g
- Protein: 27.9g

CITRUS BEEF RIBS WITH LOUISIANA HOT SAUCE

Preparation time: 25 minutes + marinating time | Cooking time: 1 hour & 10 minutes
Griddle Temperature: medium-high heat | Servings: 6-10

Ingredients:

- 2 to 3 racks of beef ribs
- 2 cups orange juice
- ½ cup extra virgin olive oil
- ½ cup balsamic vinegar
- ½ cup Worcestershire sauce
- 1 tablespoon garlic salt
- 1 tablespoon dry mustard

- 1 teaspoon paprika
- 1 teaspoon chili powder
- 1 teaspoon Louisiana Hot Sauce

Directions:

1. Preheat grill to medium-high heat. Turn on burners on one side of the griddle only. You will cook meat on the side of the grill away from heat.
2. Peel off the membrane on the backside of the rack for more tender ribs using a towel or paper towel to grip the membrane.
3. Mix all remaining ingredients, except ribs, in a large bowl. Place the ribs in a dish or Ziploc bag, pour in marinade, and marinate in the refrigerator for 4-6 hours.
4. Reserving the marinade, drain ribs, and set them aside until they reach room temperature. Place marinade in a medium saucepan and boil for at least 10 minutes. Remove from heat, cool, and reserve.
5. Cook ribs on oiled grill over medium-high (450° to 550°) over indirect heat for 1 hour, basting very frequently with the marinade.
6. Remove ribs from grill and place ribs on heavy-duty aluminum foil, baste both sides lavishly, seal foil, and set aside for 10-15 minutes to cool and become infused with marinade. Open foil packages at the table and dig in.

Nutrition:

- Calories: 350
- Carbs: 2g
- Fat: 10g
- Protein: 20g

SWEET GRIDDLE PORK RIBS

Preparation time: 10 minutes | Cooking time: 4 minutes | Griddle
Temperature: medium-high | Servings: 6

Ingredients:

- 3 pounds (1.4 kg) country-style pork ribs
- 1 cup low-sugar ketchup
- ½ cup water
- ¼ cup onion, finely chopped
- ¼ cup cider vinegar or wine vinegar
- ¼ cup light molasses
- 2 tablespoons Worcestershire sauce
- 2 teaspoons chili powder
- 2 cloves garlic, minced

Directions:

1. Combine ketchup, water, onion, vinegar, molasses, Worcestershire

sauce, chili powder, and garlic in a saucepan and bring to boil; reduce heat.

2. Simmer, uncovered, within 10 to 15 minutes or until desired thickness is reached, stirring often. Trim fat from ribs. Preheat griddle to medium-high.

3. Place ribs, bone-side down, griddle, and cook for 1-½ to 2 hours or until tender, occasionally brushing with sauce during the last 10 minutes of cooking. Serve with remaining sauce and enjoy!

Nutrition:

- Calories: 235
- Carbs: 8g
- Fat: 14g
- Protein: 19g

SALTY BEEF STEAK

Preparation time: 8 minutes | Cooking time: 15 minutes | Griddle
Temperature: high heat | Servings: 4

Ingredients:

- 2 porterhouse steaks, about 1½ inches thick
- Butcher's salt, for coating

Directions:

1. Wipe the griddle using oil to prevent sticking, set it to high heat. Pat your steaks dry and coat with the salt. Let sit for 20 to 30 minutes. Place the steaks over high heat.
2. Cook within 2 minutes, then turn the steaks 45 degrees and cook for another 2 minutes. Flip and repeat on the other side.
3. Cook, occasionally flipping, within 8 to 10 minutes. Transfer it to your cutting board and let rest for 10 minutes before slicing and serving.

Nutrition:

- Calories: 116
- Carbs: 0g
- Fat: 3g
- Protein: 23g

PEPPERY STRIP STEAK

Preparation time: 45 minutes | Cooking time: 8 minutes | Griddle
Temperature: medium-high | Servings: 1

Ingredients:

- 1 (8 ounces) NY strip steak
- Olive oil, as needed
- Sea salt & ground black pepper, to taste

Directions:

1. Preheat griddle to medium-high heat and brush with olive oil. Flavor the steak on all sides with salt and pepper—Cook steak for about 4 to 5 minutes.
2. Flip and cook within 4 minutes more for medium-rare steak; between 125°F and 130°F on a meat thermometer. Transfer your steak to a plate, then let it rest for 5 minutes before serving.

Nutrition:

- Calories: 290
- Carbs: 0g
- Fat: 22g
- Protein: 21g

CHEESY GRIDDLE PIZZA

Preparation time: 10 minutes | Cooking time: 20 minutes | Griddle
Temperature: medium heat | Servings: 4

Ingredients:

- 8 slices French bread
- 3 tablespoons butter, softened
- 1/2 cup pizza sauce
- 1/4 cup mozzarella cheese
- 1/2 cup pepperoni diced
- Garlic powder for dusting
- Oregano, for dusting

Directions:

1. Spread your butter on one side of each French bread slice. Place butter

side down on a piece of aluminum foil and dust with garlic powder and oregano.
2. Spread pizza sauce on the opposite side of all French bread slices. Top 4 slices of bread with mozzarella cheese, a few slices of pepperoni, and additional mozzarella.
3. Place the rest of your French bread slices on top of pizza topped bread, butter side up, to create 4 sandwiches.
4. Preheat the griddle to medium heat and place one slice of bread, buttered side down into the griddle.
5. Cook within 3 minutes and flip to cook 3 minutes on the other side; cook until bread is golden and cheese is melted. Serve warm and enjoy!

Nutrition:

- Calories: 305
- Fat: 12g
- Carbs: 40.4g
- Protein: 9.4g

CHICKEN WITH ROOT BEER

Preparation time: 5 minutes + marinating time | Cooking time: 20 minutes | Griddle Temperature: medium-high heat | Servings: 4

Ingredients:

- 1 lb. boneless chicken thighs
- 1 (12 ounces) cans root beer,
- Olive oil, as needed

For the rub:

- 1 tablespoon garlic powder
- 3/4 tablespoon sea salt
- 1/2 tablespoon white pepper
- 2 teaspoons smoked paprika
- 2 teaspoons garlic powder

- 1 teaspoon dried thyme
- 1/8 teaspoon cayenne pepper

Directions:

1. Combine rub ingredients in a bowl; reserve half in a separate air-tight container until ready to cook.   Rub chicken thighs evenly with olive oil and coat each with some rub.
2. Lay chicken in a 13 by 9-inch baking dish. Cover with 2 cans of root beer—Preheat griddle to medium-high heat.
3. Discard marinade and brush griddle with olive oil. Gently fold the remaining rub and a half of the third can of root beer in a small bowl.
4. Sear chicken for 7 minutes on each side, often basting with root beer rub mix. Serve when cooked through, or the chicken reaches 165°F and juices run clear.

Nutrition:

- Calories: 363
- Fat: 12.1g
- Carbs: 29.9g
- Protein: 33.4g

YELLOW CHICKEN WINGS CURRY

Preparation time: 5 minutes + chilling time| Cooking time: 30-60 minutes |
Griddle Temperature: medium-heat | Servings: 6

Ingredients:

- 2 lbs. chicken wings

For the marinade:

- 1/2 cup Greek yogurt, plain
- tablespoon mild yellow curry powder
- tablespoon olive oil
- ½ teaspoon sea salt
- ½ teaspoon black pepper
- 1 teaspoon red chili flakes

Directions:

1. Rinse and pat wings dry with paper towels. Whisk marinade ingredients together in a large mixing bowl until well-combined. Add wings to

bowl and toss to coat.

2. Cover bowl with plastic wrap and chill in the refrigerator for 30 minutes. Preparation time is one side of the griddle for medium heat and the other side on medium-high.

3. Working in batches, griddle wings over medium heat, occasionally turning, until the skin starts to brown; about 12 minutes.

4. Move wings to the medium-high area of the griddle for 5 minutes on each side to char until cooked through; the meat thermometer should register 165°F when touching the bone. Transfer wings to a platter and serve warm.

Nutrition:

- Calories: 324
- Fat: 14g
- Carbs: 1.4g
- Protein: 45.6g

LOBSTER TAILS WITH BASIL & BUTTER

Preparation time: 5 minutes | Cooking time: 6 minutes | Griddle Temperature: medium-high heat| Servings: 4

Ingredients:

- 4 lobster tails (cut in half lengthwise)
- 3 tablespoons olive oil
- lime wedges (to serve)
- Sea salt, to taste

The Lime Basil Butter:

- 1 stick unsalted butter, softened
- ½ bunch basil, roughly chopped

- 1 lime, zested and juiced
- 2 cloves garlic, minced
- ¼ teaspoon red pepper flakes

Directions:

1. Add the butter ingredients to a mixing bowl and combine; set aside until ready to use—Preheat griddle to medium-high heat.
2. Drizzle the lobster tail halves with olive oil and season with salt and pepper. Place the lobster tails, flesh-side down, on the griddle.
3. Allow to cook until opaque, about 3 minutes, flip and cook another 3 minutes. Add a dollop of the lime basil butter during the last minute of cooking. Serve immediately.

Nutrition:

- Calories: 180
- Carbs: 0g
- Fat: 7g
- Protein: 23g

DIJON MUSTARD TENDER PORK LOIN

Preparation time: 10 minutes | Cooking time: 4 hours | Griddle Temperature: medium heat | Servings: 6

Ingredients:

- 2 1 lb. pork tenderloins
- 2 tablespoons Dijon mustard
- 1 1/2 teaspoons smoked paprika
- 1 teaspoon salt
- 2 tablespoons olive oil

Directions:

1. Mix the mustard and paprika in a small bowl. Set your griddle to medium heat. Rub the tenderloins with the mustard mixture, making sure they are evenly coated.
2. Place the tenderloins on the griddle and cook until all sides are well

browned, and the internal temperature is 135°F.

3. Remove the tenderloins from the griddle and rest 5 minutes before slicing and serving.

Nutrition:

- Calories: 484
- Fat: 24.7g
- Carbs:13.8g
- Protein: 50.9g

HAKKA NOODLES WITH SMOKED PORK SAUSAGE

Preparation time: 5 minutes | Cooking time: 27 minutes | Griddle
Temperature: medium heat | Servings: 5

Ingredients:

- 1 packet Hakka noodles
- 5 smoked pork sausages
- 50g coriander leaves
- 1 tbsp. soya sauce
- 50g mint leaves
- 1 onion
- 3 green chilies
- 1 capsicum
- salt to taste

Directions:

1. Cut and slice all the pork vegetables and keep them aside. Then cook the packet of Hakka noodle in a container. Make sure to add a little bit of oil so that they don't stick together. Boil the noodles for 5-6 minutes.
2. Take the noodles and transfer them to a strainer and wash them under the tap to stop cooking.
3. Then add a little bit of oil and soya sauce to the noodles. Once this is ready, we are ready to cook the rest of the meal.
4. Prepare griddle for medium heat. Lightly oil. Add the onions and chilies till they turn light brown. Then add the smoked pork sausages and cook it for 5 – 7 minutes.
5. Add the coriander and mint leaves and cook for another 5 minutes. The major aroma will be from the coriander and mint leaves.
6. Then add the cauliflower, capsicum, and salt to taste. Then add the noodles and then cook it for another 5 minutes. Take it off the griddle and then serve it with mint leaves.

Nutrition:

- Calories 220
- Protein 25.7 g
- Carbs 33.2 g
- Fat 23g

COGNAC STEAKS WITH SHITAKE MUSHROOMS

Preparation time: 5 minutes | Cooking time: 21 minutes | Griddle
Temperature: highest heat | Servings: 6

Ingredients:

- 1 tablespoon extra-virgin olive oil
- ½ cup very finely chopped shallots
- ½ cup thinly sliced green onions
- ½ cup chopped shitake mushrooms
- 1/8 cup cognac

- ¼ teaspoon salt
- ¼ teaspoon pepper
- 2 boneless beef top loin steaks, cut 2-inches thick, about 1 pound each
- wooden toothpicks, soaked for 20 minutes in hot water

Directions:

1. In a small non-stick skillet, heat oil over medium heat until hot. Add shallots and mushrooms and cook 4-5 minutes or until tender.
2. Then add green onions and continue grilling and stirring 4-5 minutes or until onions are tender. Remove from heat. Add the salt, pepper, and cognac, and cool completely.
3. Meanwhile, with a sharp knife, make a pocket in each steak by cutting horizontally along one long side to within ½-inch of each of the other 3 sides.
4. Spread half of mixture inside each pocket. Secure the pockets with 2 or 3 wooden toothpicks.
5. Place 2"-inch thick steaks on the griddle grill while flipping the steaks after 6 to 8 minutes per side. Remove wooden toothpicks. Carve steaks crosswise into ½-inch thick slices. Serve.

Nutrition:

- Calories: 159
- Carbs: 2g
- Fat: 7g
- Protein: 21g

COUNTRY-STYLE GLAZED RIBS

Preparation time: 25 minutes | Cooking time: 2 hours & 15 minutes | Griddle
Temperature: medium-high | Servings: 6

Ingredients:

- 3 pounds country-style pork ribs
- 1 cup low-sugar ketchup
- ½ cup water
- ¼ cup onion, finely chopped
- ¼ cup cider vinegar or wine vinegar
- ¼ cup light molasses
- 2 tablespoons Worcestershire sauce
- 2 teaspoons chili powder
- 2 cloves garlic, minced

Directions:

1. Combine ketchup, water, onion, vinegar, molasses, Worcestershire sauce, chili powder, and garlic in a saucepan and bring to boil; reduce

heat.

2. Simmer, uncovered, within 10 to 15 minutes or until desired thickness is reached, stirring often. Trim fat from ribs. Preheat griddle to medium-high.

3. Place ribs, bone-side down, griddle, and cook for 1-1/2 to 2 hours or until tender, occasionally brushing with sauce during the last 10 minutes of cooking. Serve with remaining sauce and enjoy!

Nutrition:

- Calories: 404
- Fat: 8.1g
- Carbs:15.2g
- Protein: 60.4g

SKIRT STEAK WITH COFFEE RUBBED

Preparation time: 15 minutes | Cooking time: 20 minutes | Griddle
Temperature: high | Servings: 8

Ingredients:

- 1/4 cup coffee beans, finely ground
- 1/4 cup dark brown sugar
- 1 1/2 teaspoon sea salt
- 1/8 teaspoon ground cinnamon
- Pinch of cayenne pepper
- 2 1/2 lb. skirt steak, slice into 4 pieces
- 1 tablespoon olive oil

Directions:

1. Heat griddle to high. Combine coffee, brown sugar, salt, cinnamon, and cayenne pepper in a bowl to make a rub.
2. Remove steak from your fridge and let come to room temperature, about 15 minutes. Rub steak with oil, and sprinkle with spice rub. Massage spice rub into meat.
3. Sear until charred and medium-rare within 2 to 4 minutes per side. Transfer to a cutting board, cover with foil, and let rest 5 minutes before thinly slicing against the grain.

Nutrition:

- Calories:324
- Fat: 16g
- Carbs: 4.6g
- Protein: 37.9g

CORN HONEY-LIME TILAPIA

Preparation time: 10 minutes | Cooking time: 10 minutes | Griddle
Temperature: high | Servings: 4

Ingredients:

- 4 fillets tilapia
- 2 tablespoons honey
- 4 limes, thinly sliced
- 2 ears corn, shucked
- 2 tablespoons fresh cilantro leaves
- 1/4 cup olive oil
- Kosher salt
- Freshly ground black pepper

Directions:

1. Preheat griddle to high. Cut 4 squares of foil about 12" long. Put a piece of tilapia on each piece of foil. Brush tilapia using honey and top with

lime, corn, and cilantro.

2. Drizzle with olive oil, then flavor it with sea salt plus pepper. Cook until tilapia is cooked through and corn tender, about 15 minutes.

Nutrition:

- Calories: 319
- Fat: 14.7g
- Carbs: 30.3g
- Protein: 24g

PINEAPPLE SHRIMP SKEWERS

Preparation time: 20 minutes | Cooking time: 5 minutes | Griddle
Temperature: medium heat | Servings: 4

Ingredients:

- 1½ pounds uncooked jumbo shrimp, peeled and deveined
- ½ cup light coconut milk
- 1 tablespoon cilantro, chopped
- 4 teaspoons Tabasco Original Red Sauce
- 2 teaspoons soy sauce
- ¼ cup freshly squeezed orange juice
- ¼ cup freshly squeezed lime juice (from about 2 large limes)
- ¾ pound pineapple, cut into 1-inch chunks
- Olive oil for grilling

Directions:

1. Combine the coconut milk, cilantro, Tabasco sauce, soy sauce, orange juice, lime juice. Add the shrimp and toss to coat.
2. Cover then place in your refrigerator to marinate for 1 hour. Thread

shrimp and pineapple onto metal skewers, alternating each—Preheat griddle to medium heat.

3. Cook 5-6 minutes, flipping once, until shrimp turn opaque pink. Serve immediately.

Nutrition:

- Calories: 279
- Carbs: 43g
- Fat: 2g
- Protein: 25g

SHRIMP SKEWERS WITH PESTO PISTACHIO

Preparation time: 35 minutes | Cooking time: 6 minutes | Griddle
Temperature: medium heat | Servings: 4

Ingredients:

- 1-1/2 lb. Uncooked shrimp, peeled and deveined
- 2 tablespoons lemon juice
- 1/4 cup Parmesan cheese, shredded
- 1/4 teaspoon of sea salt
- 1/8 teaspoon black ground pepper
- 1/2 cup olive oil
- 1/2 cup parsley, fresh minced
- 1 garlic clove, peeled
- 1/3 cup pistachios, shelled
- 1/4 teaspoon grated lemon zest
- 3/4 cup arugula, fresh

Directions:

1. Put the olive oil, lemon zest, garlic clove, pistachios, parsley, arugula, and lemon juice to a blender. Blend until smooth.
2. Add your Parmesan cheese, sea salt, and pepper, then mix well. Toss in your shrimp and allow to marinate in the fridge for 30 minutes. Thread your shrimp onto skewers.
3. Preheat your griddle grill on the medium temperature setting. Once preheated, add your skewers onto the grill and close the lid. Grill for 6 minutes. Rotate the skewers every 2 minutes. Serve and enjoy!

Nutrition:

- Calories: 293
- Fat: 16g
- Carbs: 5.2g
- Protein: 34.2g

LEMON HALIBUT FILLETS WITH DILL, SPINACH & OLIVES

Preparation time: 10 minutes | Cooking time: 12 minutes | Griddle
Temperature: medium heat | Servings: 4

Ingredients:

- 4 (6 ounces) halibut fillets
- 1/3 cup olive oil
- 4 cups baby spinach
- 1/4 cup lemon juice
- 2 ounces pitted black olives, halved
- 2 tablespoons flat-leaf parsley, chopped
- 2 teaspoons fresh dill, chopped
- Lemon wedges, to serve

Directions:

1. Preheat griddle to medium heat. Toss spinach with lemon juice in a

mixing bowl and set aside. Brush fish with olive oil and cook for 3-4 minutes per side or until cooked through.
2.   Remove from heat, cover with foil and let rest for 5 minutes. Add remaining oil and cook spinach for 2 minutes, or until just wilted. Remove from heat.
3.   Toss with olives and herbs, then transfer to serving plates with fish, and serve with lemon wedges.

Nutrition:

- Calories: 773
- Fat: 36.6g
- Carbs: 2.9g
- Protein: 109.3g

SPICY RED SNAPPER FILLETS

Preparation time: 10 minutes | Cooking time: 8 minutes | Griddle
Temperature: high heat | Servings: 2

Ingredients:

- 2 red snapper fish fillets
- 1 tbsp olive oil
- 1 tsp chili powder
- 1/2 tsp pepper
- 1/2 tsp garlic powder
- 1/2 tsp onion powder
- 1 tbsp paprika
- 1/2 tsp salt

Directions:

1. In a small bowl, mix chili powder, pepper, garlic powder, onion powder, paprika, and salt. Brush fish fillets with oil and rub with spice

mixture—Preheat the Griddle to high heat.

2. Place fish fillets on a hot griddle top and cook for 3-4 minutes on each side. Serve and enjoy.

Nutrition:

- Calories 110
- Fat 8.2 g
- Carbohydrates 9.5 g
- Protein 1.9 g

RAINBOW TROUT WITH CUMIN AND BURNT CITRUS VINAIGRETTE

Preparation time: 7 minutes | Cooking time: 15 minutes | Griddle
Temperature: medium-high heat | Servings: 4

Ingredients:

- 4 whole rainbow trout, 12 to 16 ounces each, scaled and gutted
- Oil and salt, for coating
- Cumin and Burnt Citrus Vinaigrette:
- 1½ tablespoons cumin seeds
- 3 oranges
- 3 lemons
- 1½ cups oil, plus more for coating
- 3 tablespoons honey, plus more for coating
- ¼ cup vinegar
- ½ shallot, grated
- 1½ teaspoons salt

- ½ teaspoon Mexican oregano

Directions:

1. Preheat griddle to medium-high heat and brush with olive oil.
2. For the vinaigrette, add the cumin to Griddle and shake over medium heat until toasted and fragrant, about 2 minutes. Grind until very fine in a spice grinder or blender and set aside.
3. Zest 1 orange and 1 lemon and set zest aside. Slice all the oranges plus lemons in half and toss in about 1 tablespoon each of oil and honey, just enough to coat.
4. Place the citrus cut side down on the griddle over medium heat and grill until nicely charred and fragrant, 1 to 2 minutes. Once they have cooled, juice to get about 1½ cups juice.
5. Combine the juice, vinegar, shallot, orange and lemon zest, cumin, salt, oregano, and remaining 2 tablespoons honey in a bowl. Whisk until the salt plus honey have dissolved.
6. While whisking, slowly pour in the 1½ cup oil and continue to whisk until emulsified. The vinaigrette can be stored in a covered container in the refrigerator for up to 1 week.
7. For the trout, open and gently press each fish, so it lies flat. Rub the fish with oil and salt. Place skin side down over medium heat and cook until the skin is browned and crisp, and the flesh turns opaque 4 to 5 minutes. Serve the fish folded back over.

Nutrition:

- Calories: 176
- Carbs: 31g
- Fat: 4g
- Protein: 5g

CHILI CRAB LEGS

Preparation time: 5 minutes | Cooking time: 5 minutes | Griddle Temperature: high heat | Servings: 4

Ingredients:

- 4 lb. king crab legs, cooked
- 2 tablespoons chili oil

Directions:

1. Preheat griddle to high. Brush both sides of crab legs with chili oil and place on grill. Tent with foil. Cook 4 to 5 minutes, turning once. Transfer to plates and serve with drawn butter.

Nutrition:

- Calories: 518
- Fat: 13.9g
- Carbs: 0g
- Protein: 87.1g

CHILI GRILLED SHRIMP

Preparation time: 15 minutes | Cooking time: 8 minutes | Griddle
Temperature: medium heat | Servings: 6

Ingredients:

- 1-1/2 pounds uncooked jumbo shrimp, peeled and deveined

For the marinade:

- 2 tablespoons fresh parsley
- 1 bay leaf, dried
- 1 teaspoon chili powder
- 1 teaspoon garlic powder
- 1/4 teaspoon cayenne pepper
- 1/4 cup olive oil
- 1/4 teaspoon salt
- 1/8 teaspoon pepper

Directions:

1. Add marinade fixings to a food processor and process until smooth—transfer marinade to a large mixing bowl. Fold in shrimp and toss to coat; refrigerate, covered, 30 minutes.
2. Thread shrimp onto metal skewers. Preheat griddle to medium heat. Cook 5-6 minutes, flipping once, until shrimp turn opaque pink. Serve immediately.

Nutrition:

- Calories: 131
- Fat: 8.5g
- Carbs: 1g
- Protein: 13.7g

OYSTERS WITH TEQUILA INFUSED CHILI BUTTER

Preparation time: 5 minutes | Cooking time: 25 minutes | Griddle
Temperature: high heat | Servings: 6

Ingredients:

- 3 dozen medium oysters, scrubbed and shucked
- Flakey sea salt, for serving

For the butter:

- 1/4 teaspoon crushed red pepper
- 7 tablespoons unsalted butter
- ¼ teaspoon chili oil
- 1 teaspoon dried oregano
- 2 tablespoons freshly squeezed lemon juice

- 2 tablespoons tequila Blanco

Directions:

1. Combine butter ingredients in a small mixing bowl until well incorporated and set aside. Preheat griddle to high. Grill the oysters for about 1 to 2 minutes.
2. Sprinkle the oysters with salt flakes. Warm the butter in a microwave for 30 seconds, and spoon the warm tequila butter over the oysters and serve.

Nutrition:

- Calories: 184
- Fat: 15g
- Carbs: 3.8g
- Protein: 0.2g

OCTOPUS WITH HERBS & LEMON

Preparation time: 5 minutes | Cooking time: 10 minutes | Griddle
Temperature: high heat | Servings: 4

Ingredients:

- 3 lemons, 1 halved
- 3 pounds cleaned octopus, thawed if frozen
- 6 cloves garlic, peeled
- 4 sprigs of fresh oregano
- 2 bay leaves
- Salt and pepper
- 3 tablespoons good-quality olive oil
- Minced fresh oregano for garnish

Directions:

1. Put the octopus, garlic, oregano sprigs, bay leaves, a large pinch of salt, and lemon halves in a large pot with enough water to cover by a couple

of inches.

2. Bring to a boil, adjust the heat so the liquid bubbles gently but steadily, and cook, occasionally turning with tongs, until the octopus is tender 30 to 90 minutes. Drain; discard the seasonings.

3. Squeeze the juice 1 of the remaining lemons and whisk it with the oil and salt and pepper to taste. Cut the octopus into large serving pieces and toss with the oil mixture.

4. Bring the griddle grill to high heat. Oil the Griddle. Put the octopus on the grill, and cook until heated through and charred, 4 to 5 minutes per side.

5. Cut the remaining lemon into wedges. Transfer the octopus to a platter, sprinkle with minced oregano, and serve with the lemon wedges.

Nutrition:

- Calories: 105
- Carbs: 19g
- Fat: 2g
- Protein: 3g

GRIDDLE SPICE CHICKPEAS

Preparation time: 5 minutes | Cooking time: 30 minutes | Griddle
Temperature: medium heat | Servings: 2

Ingredients:

- 1 (16-ounce) can chickpeas, drained
- ¼ cup olive oil
- 1 tablespoon ground cumin
- 1 tablespoon smoked paprika
- 1 teaspoon garlic powder
- 1 teaspoon onion powder
- 1 teaspoon kosher salt, + more to taste

Directions:

1. Combine all ingredients in a large bowl. Pour the mixture onto a cool griddle grill and bring the Griddle to medium heat.
2. Allow the mixture to slowly come to temperature and continue to cook,

frequently stirring, for up to 30 minutes or until the garbanzo beans have lost most of their moisture and become crispy and crunchy. Finish with additional salt, if desired.

Nutrition:

- Calories: 160
- Carbs: 21g
- Fat: 5g
- Protein: 6g

PORK CHOPS WITH HERBS

Preparation time: 5 minutes | Cooking time: 7-8 minutes | Griddle
Temperature: medium heat | Servings: 4

Ingredients:

- 2 tbsps. Kosher salt
- 8 large basil leaves, torn into pieces
- 2 stems fresh rosemary, crushed
- 2 tbsp thyme leaves, crushed
- 3 cloves garlic, diced
- 1 tbsps. salt
- 4 thick-cut bone-in pork chops, 1-inch thick

Directions:

1. Mix the salt, basil, rosemary, thyme, garlic, plus pepper in a small bowl. Rub this batter over your pork chops until thoroughly covered.
2. Prepare Griddle for medium heat. Lightly oil. Place on Griddle. Cook

within 7-8 minutes, turning once. Cover with basting cover.

3. Put a little water on your surface before you cover. If your chops are thinner or thicker than 1", adjust the cooking time accordingly.

4. Remove chops from heat, cover, and let rest for 3 - 5 minutes before serving. Serve with a summer vegetable medley and top with a pat of compound butter seasoned with the same herbs used in the rub.

Nutrition:

- Calories 221
- Fat 11g
- Carbs 1g
- Protein 26g

TORTILLA WEDGES WITH FIRE-ROASTED TOMATILLO SALSA

Preparation time: 5 minutes | Cooking time: 10 minutes | Griddle
Temperature: high heat | Servings: 2 cups

Ingredients:

- 1 pound tomatillos
- 3 scallions, trimmed
- 1 jalapeño chili, seeded and minced
- 2 cloves garlic, minced, or to taste
- ¼ cup chopped fresh cilantro
- 3 tbsp fresh lime juice, or to taste
- Salt and pepper
- 8 small corn or flour tortillas
- olive oil for brushing

Directions:

1. Remove the husks from the tomatillos, then rinse off the tacky residue and pat dry. Bring the griddle grill to high heat. Oil the griddle.
2. Put the tomatillos and scallions on the grill, and cook until they soften and blacken in spots, turning them to cook evenly, 5 to 10 minutes total.
3. Transfer to a food processor or blender and add the jalapeño, garlic, cilantro, lime juice, salt, and pepper; pulse a few times. Taste and adjust your seasoning, adding more garlic or lime if you like.
4. Brush the tortillas on both sides with oil. Put them on the grill directly over the fire, close the lid, and toast, turning once until they are warm and grill marks develop, 1 to 2 minutes per side. Slice into wedges, then serve with the salsa.

Nutrition:

- Calories: 180
- Carbs: 28g
- Fat: 5g
- Protein: 5g

TACO PIÑA COLADA WITH COCONUT

Preparation time: 35 minutes | Cooking time: 24 minutes | Griddle Temperature: medium heat | Servings: 4

Ingredients:

- ½ ripe pineapple, peeled, cored, & cut into 1-inch cubes
- ¼ cup dark rum
- ¼ cup coconut milk
- 4 tablespoons (½ stick) butter, softened
- 4 7-inch flour tortillas
- 1 tablespoon sugar, or as needed
- Lime wedges for serving (optional)
- ½ cup shredded coconut, toasted

Directions:

1. Place the pineapple, rum, and coconut milk in a bowl and toss to combine. Let the fruit macerate within 20 minutes or up to several hours in the refrigerator.
2. Heat your griddle to medium heat. Spread the butter on all sides of the tortillas, then sprinkle with the sugar. Thread the pineapple cubes onto 4 skewers, letting excess marinade drip back in the bowl.
3. Place the skewers on the grill directly. Cook until the pineapple is caramelized, 5 to 10 minutes per side, depending on how hot it is.
4. Transfer the skewers to a platter. Place the tortillas on the grill directly, cook turning once, until they are lightly brown, 1 to 2 minutes per side.
5. To serve, Place a skewer on top of each tortilla, squeeze with some lime if you like, and sprinkle with toasted coconut. To eat, pull out the skewer.

Nutrition:

- Calories: 170
- Carbs: 36g
- Fat: 4g
- Protein: 0g

GRILLED CARAMEL ORANGES

Preparation time: 10 minutes | Cooking time: 13 minutes | Griddle
Temperature: medium heat | Servings: 4

Ingredients:

- ¼ cup sugar
- ½ teaspoon five-spice powder
- 2 large oranges
- ¼ cup chopped fresh mint

Directions:

1. Mix the sugar and five-spice powder on a small plate. Slice a sliver off the top and bottom of each orange so that it will sit flat on the grates without rolling, then turn them on their sides and cut in half through the equator. Remove any seeds.
2. Press the cut side of each half into the sugar. Let sit until the sugar is absorbed and you are ready to grill. Heat your griddle to medium heat. Place the orange halves on the grill directly, sugared side up.

3. Until they are warm throughout, 5 to 10 minutes, turn them over and cook just until the cut sides brown, 2 to 3 minutes.
4. Transfer to individual serving plates, sprinkle with the mint and serve with a knife and fork or with grapefruit spoons if you have them.

Nutrition:

- Calories: 90
- Carbs: 20g
- Fat: 0g
- Protein: 1g

GRILLED SWISS CREPES WITH HAM

Preparation time: 15 minutes | Cooking time: 25 minutes | Griddle Temperature: medium heat | Servings: 2

Ingredients:

- 2 tablespoons oil
- ½ red bell pepper, thinly sliced
- 6 thin slices of Black Forest ham
- 4 thin slices of Swiss cheese
- 2 prepared crepes
- 2 teaspoons Dijon mustard

Directions:

1. Bring the griddle grill to medium and heat the oil. Sauté the bell pepper strips for 5 to 7 minutes, until wilted. Set aside and keep warm.

2. Spread ham slices out on the griddle grill and warm them for about 5 minutes on one side. Flip the ham and arrange it into two piles of three slices, letting the slices overlap.
3. Put two slices of cheese on each of the piles of ham, add a few tablespoons of water to the Griddle, and cover to help the cheese melt.
4. While the cheese is melting, warm the crepes on the Griddle and spread half the mustard on each. Top with the ham and melted cheese and sautéed bell peppers. Fold and serve.

Nutrition:

- Calories: 240
- Carbs: 21g
- Fat: 10g
- Protein: 17g

GRILLED MUSHROOMS WITH ROSEMARY

Preparation time: 5 minutes | Cooking time: 20 minutes | Griddle
Temperature: medium heat | Servings: 4

Ingredients:

- 4 large portobello mushrooms, or 1½ pounds shiitake, button, or cremini mushrooms
- 1/3 cup good-quality olive oil
- 1 tablespoon minced shallot, scallion, onion, or garlic
- 1 tablespoon chopped fresh rosemary
- Salt and pepper, as needed

Directions:

1. Heat a griddle for medium heat. Rinse and trim the mushrooms to remove any tough stems. Combine the oil, shallot, rosemary, and some

salt and pepper in a small bowl.

2. Brush your mushrooms all over with about half of the mixture; reserve the rest. Skewer the mushrooms if they're small or place them in a perforated grill pan.

3. Place the mushrooms on the grill directly. Cook while turning or shaking the pan to cook evenly until they soften and a knife pierces the center with no resistance, 5 to 20 minutes.

4. Brush with the remaining oil as they cook. Transfer to a platter. Portobellos can be served whole or cut into wedges or slices. All are good hot, warm, or at room temperature.

Nutrition:

- Calories: 87
- Carbs: 8g
- Fat: 3g
- Protein: 7g

GRILLED BUTTERNUT SQUASH WITH MELTED BUTTER

Preparation time: 5 minutes | Cooking time: 60 minutes | Griddle
Temperature: medium-high heat | Servings: 4

Ingredients:

- 2 pounds butternut squash, cut into large pieces, and seeded
- 4 tablespoons (½ stick) butter, melted
- Salt and pepper

Directions:

1. Heat a griddle for medium-high heat. Brush the cut sides of your squash with about half of the melted butter, then sprinkle with salt and pepper.
2. Place the squash on the grill directly, skin side down. Cook until a skewer can be inserted through the center of each chunk without resistance, about 1 hour depending on their thickness.

3. Transfer to a cutting board. Slice the blackened skin, then cut the squash into bite-sized cubes.
4. Place in a serving bowl and spry with the remaining melted butter. Taste and adjust the seasoning, toss to combine, and serve.

Nutrition:

- Calories: 272
- Carbs: 71g
- Fat: 1g
- Protein: 6g

DESSERTS

HONEY GRILLED PEACHES

Preparation time: 5 minutes | Cooking time: 5 minutes | Griddle Temperature: medium-low heat | Servings: 4

Ingredients:

- fresh peaches, as desired
- fresh honey, as desired
- cinnamon to taste
- coconut oil, as needed
- plain yogurt or ice cream for topping

Directions:

1. Slice the peaches lengthwise top to bottom and remove the pits. Drizzle honey on the cut side of the peach and sprinkle with cinnamon.
2. Bring the griddle grill to medium-low heat. Oil the Griddle and allow it to heat until the oil is shimmering but not smoking.
3. Set the peaches sliced-side up and grill peaches for a couple of minutes

cut side down, then flip and brush with coconut oil honey, and cinnamon
4. Grill for several minutes until the skin is starting to brown and pull back. Serve with vanilla ice cream while still warm.

Nutrition:

- Calories: 132
- Carbs: 32g
- Fat: 0g
- Protein: 13g

ROSEMARY WATERMELON STEAKS

Preparation time: 5 minutes | Cooking time: 10 minutes | Griddle
Temperature: medium heat | Servings: 4-8

Ingredients:

- 1 small watermelon, removed seeds
- ¼ cup good-quality olive oil
- 1 tablespoon minced fresh rosemary
- Salt and pepper, as needed
- Lemon wedges for serving

Directions:

1. Heat a griddle for medium heat. Cut the watermelon into 2-inch-thick slices, with the rind intact, and then into halves or quarters, if you like.
2. Place the oil and rosemary in a small bowl, sprinkle with salt and pepper, and stir. Brush or rub this batter all over the watermelon slices.

3. Place the watermelon on the grill directly. Cook turning once until the flesh develops grill marks and has dried out a bit, 4 to 5 minutes per side. Transfer it to your platter and serve with lemon wedges.

Nutrition:

- Calories: 101
- Carbs: 11g
- Fat: 0g
- Protein: 2g

BANANA CINNAMON COCONUT FRITTERS

Preparation time: 5 minutes | Cooking time: 4 minutes | Griddle Temperature: medium heat | Servings: 12 fritters

Ingredients:

- 2 bananas, mashed
- 1/3 cup flour
- ½ tsp. cinnamon
- 2 eggs
- ½ cup shredded coconut

Directions:

1. Combine all fixings except oil in a bowl—Preheat griddle pan for 4 minutes on medium heat. Coat the pan with canola oil. Drop heaping tablespoons of fritter batter onto the pan. Serve.

Nutrition:

- Calories: 115
- Carbs: 11g
- Fat: 7g
- Protein: 2g

GRILLED PINEAPPLE DISK WITH VANILLA BEAN ICE CREAM

Preparation time: 5 minutes | Cooking time: 4 minutes | Griddle Temperature: medium-low heat | Servings: 4

Ingredients:

- 1 whole pineapple, sliced into 6 equal slices
- 6 scoops of vanilla bean ice cream
- 6 spoonsful of whipped cream
- ¼ cup almond slivers, toasted
- ¼ cup sweetened shredded coconut, toasted
- ½ cup caramel sauce
- mint (to garnish)

Directions:

1. Bring the griddle grill to medium-low heat. Oil your griddle and allow it to heat until the oil is shimmering but not smoking. Grill pineapple until

a nice char forms, about 2 minutes per side.

2. Remove pineapple from the grill, top each slice with a scoop of ice cream, a dollop of whipped cream, almonds, and coconut. Drizzle each with caramel sauce, garnish with mint, and serve.

Nutrition:

- Calories: 140
- Carbs: 19g
- Fat: 6g
- Protein: 2g

BUTTERED POPCORN

Preparation time: 5 minutes | Cooking time: 4 minutes | Griddle Temperature: medium-high heat | Servings: 2-4

Ingredients:

- 3 tablespoons peanut oil
- ½ cup popcorn kernels
- 3 tablespoons butter
- Salt, to taste

Directions:

1. Prepare your griddle for two-zone cooking. Set the griddle grill to medium-high heat and add the peanut oil. While it is heating, place 5

popcorn kernels in the oil.

2. When 2 or 3 pop, add the butter to the oil and pour in the remaining kernels. Cover immediately with a tall pan or spaghetti pot.

3. When the popcorn starts popping, you will need to stir it in the oil to get all the kernels to pop and prevent the popped corn from burning.

4. Using insulated gloves, potholders, or thick kitchen towels, agitate the popcorn by moving the pan or pot from side to side on the griddle without lifting.

5. Cook within 4 minutes, or until the popping slows down to once every few seconds. When all the corn is popped, slide the pot or pan and popcorn to the cool side of the grill and remove the lid.

6. Use two spatulas to scoop up the hot popcorn and transfer it to a bowl. Serve with salt and additional seasonings as desired.

Nutrition:

- Calories: 170
- Carbs: 13g
- Fat: 12g
- Protein: 2g

BOURBON COCKTAIL WITH GRIDDLE BLOOD ORANGE

Preparation time: 6 minutes | Cooking time: 5 minutes | Griddle Temperature: high heat | Servings: 4

Ingredients:

- 4 blood oranges
- ¾ cup bourbon
- 1 tablespoon sugar, plus more for rimming the glasses

Directions:

1. Preheat griddle to medium-high heat and brush with olive oil. Cut 3 of the oranges in half and grill, cut side down, over high heat until charred.
2. Halve the remaining orange, cut into thick slices, and grill until charred on both sides; set aside. Squeeze the orange halves to get 1 cup of juice.
3. Add the juice, bourbon, and sugar to a cocktail shaker. Add ice to fill the shaker almost to the rim. Shake well for about 30 seconds to ensure

the sugar dissolves and the drink is well chilled.

4. Strain into a sugar-rimmed coupe or martini glasses and garnish each with a charred orange slice.

Nutrition:

- Calories: 120
- Carbs: 30g
- Fat: 0g
- Protein: 0g

CONCLUSION

If you are planning to purchase your own gas griddle do not expect any difficulties. It is a very simple process. You can do it with fewer problems by considering a few tips. You can follow the guidelines and instructions provided in this cookbook to help you purchase the best gas griddle available to you. If you follow these simple tips, you will get the best gas griddle available to you. The Blackstone Outdoor Gas Griddle can be a great choice for you. It can make your life cooler. Just remember that the Blackstone outdoor gas griddle is not a magic pill. You have to put in a little work to get the best results. Consider the reviews posted before by other Blackstone users. Do not just listen to the salesperson to buy. You can use the Blackstone griddle for several years if you want. Avoid the problem of regretting the purchase of a Blackstone griddle. Just think to yourself why you need one. Think which Blackstone griddle will be the best for you; whether it is for a big family or for simple recreational use. The size of the griddle is very important. You also have to consider your budget because a gas griddle is not as cheap as a small kitchen blender.

Do not take too much time making a choice. You have to hurry if you want the best Blackstone griddle. Take a look at the various resources available for your choice of the griddle. There are online directories that come with information regarding the various benefits of the Blackstone griddles and their varieties. You can also read the different reviews about the Blackstone griddles. Go through the description and features of the griddle that you want to purchase. It is very important for you to do it if you want the best. Then, decide about getting a griddle that fits your needs.

Just remember that there is no magic solution when you are buying a Blackstone outdoor gas griddle. Hopefully, you will buy the best Blackstone Outdoor Gas Griddle for your home or restaurant. Just do not forget to learn the characteristics of each of your Blackstone griddle. If you want a Blackstone griddle for home, go for an inexpensive griddle. If you want to have a high-end kitchen accessory then a more expensive griddle is best for you.

And finally, use this cookbook to learn more about the Blackstone Outdoor Gas Griddle and cook all the mouthwatering Blackstone Outdoor Gas Griddle recipes here so you can have the perfect meal during this grilling season.

Made in United States
Troutdale, OR
06/13/2024

20519518R00087